Soccer
Warming-up and Warming-down

Klaus Bischops/Heinz-Willi Gerards

SOCCER

WARMING-UP
& WARMING-DOWN

Meyer & Meyer Sport

Original title: Fußball, Ab- und Aufwärmen
- Aachen : Meyer & Meyer Verlag, 1998
Translated by Jean Wanko

British Library Cataloguing in Publication Data
A catalogue record for this book is available from the British Library

Bischops, Klaus/ Gerards, Heinz-Willi:
Soccer: Warming-up and Warming-down /
2nd Ed. – Oxford : Meyer & Meyer Sport (UK) Ltd., 2004
ISBN 1-84126-135-1

© 2000 by Meyer & Meyer Sport (UK) Ltd.
Aachen, Adelaide, Auckland, Budapest, Graz, Johannesburg,
Miami, Olten (CH), Oxford, Singapore, Toronto
Member of the World
Sports Publishers' Association (WSPA)
www.w-s-p-a.org
Printed and bound by: FINIDR, s. r. o., Český Těšín
ISBN 1-84126-135-1
E-Mail: verlag@m-m-sports.com
www.m-m-sports.com

CONTENTS

FOREWORD

Dear Coaches,

Only when muscles are properly warmed-up can they attain their maximum potential in competitive sport. Likewise, there is less risk of injury if one warms up before a game. Thus it is a good idea if this publication sets out this visual aspect of soccer in detail.

Warming-up work is not only absolutely essential prior to each game; indeed each unit of training must be introduced with such a programme.

Each individual performer should learn how to prepare his muscles for the forthcoming game by the right sort of exercises while he is still young.

Obviously the trainer plays a significant role in giving his players the appropriate instructions and keeping an eye on the warming-up programme.

I am therefore pleased to see that this book offers useful and important advice for all coaches.

Rainer Bonhof

(German Soccer Association Coach)

DEUTSCHER
FUSSBALL-BUND

WARMING-UP & WARMING-DOWN

No-one will believe that professional Grand Prix driver Michael Schumacher starts a race before he has warmed-up both engine and tyres. This would immediately reduce his chances of winning or gaining a place amongst the first few to nil. And how much more important is such a warming-up session in an organic being like a human being before starting any strenuous sport – and a soccer match or training lasting more than 90 to 120 minutes is exertion – so that the necessary working temperature is reached, optimal potential is achieved and danger of injury is reduced by physical and psychological preparation.

Therefore, it is unimportant whether a professional player or an amateur from a local club is doing the kicking. Everyone gets near to his own particular performance limit at times, but each and every situation demands the most careful weighing up and preparation.

With our book we should like to give both soccer trainers and exercise leaders, as well as the players themselves, some basic insight into the need for warming-up and warming-down, and thereby clarify the positive influences on both game and training. In the methodology section we want to make the theoretical background knowledge comprehensible for our readers. However, the main emphasis of our book is the 40 training units covering all the various kinds of warming-up and warming-down.

If warming-up takes place this should ensure maximum potential from the very outset of the game and can even help to score an early goal or prevent opposing goals. However, warming-up and warming-down must not be reduced to the level of any ritualistic exhibitionism, which largely covers the trainer's wishes and pacifies the crowd. Each active participant must himself be convinced of the need for pre- and post-preparation, and do it in line with his own physical and mental attitude, keeping his eye on the task ahead of him. The job of the training leader is to strengthen this attitude in the players.

Warming-up and warming-down, so that
- ▶ playing soccer is good fun,
- ▶ the game brings success,
- ▶ the risk of injury is reduced.

We, the authors, wish you success as you put our programmes into practice, and also that you enjoy playing and training with specific warming-up and warming-down.

Klaus Bischops and Heinz-Willi Gerards

1 WARMING-UP & WARMING-DOWN IN SOCCER – IS THIS A MUST?

If one watches certain professional soccer players before an important match, one may detect a certain lack of enthusiasm in their movements and reluctance to do what the trainer says. Such behaviour indicates lack of conviction of the necessity of certain actions.

Even if some players still see a bit of sense in warming-up, they regard warming-down after the game as a crackpot idea of some extrovert trainer!

In most other kinds of sport one has come a lot further with putting proven scientific theories into practice, so that a 12.0 sprinter recognises the need to warm-up before starting a 100 metre race, as also each gymnast will warm-up thoroughly before any competition and stretch, strengthen and complete some of his floor gymnastic exercises, even if he is only taking part in a local competition. This attitude is taken for granted in most kinds of sport at top-of-the-league level as well as in every competitive sportsman.

However in soccer there is still a need for convincing trainers and exercise leaders more, because the necessary warming-up and warming-down before and after each strenuous performance is in no way dependent on the level of play. No matter whether in the national or local league, it is vital to prepare properly for **each** performance. But the question still remains: "Why must I? What's the point?"

Peter RÖTHIG defines warming-up as: "An activity which brings about an optimum psycho-physical concept of training and competition." Jürgen FREIWALD divides this statement into four fundamental active principles:

> ▶ Improvement of one's general organic performance ability
> ▶ Improvement of one's co-ordinating performance ability
> ▶ Improvement of one's psychological performance ability
> ▶ Preventative precaution against injury.

With regard to warming-down one can thereby improve one's regeneration ability further.

Warming-up before training and a match can contain certain variations. Both lead to increased body and muscle temperature, but when training, the warming-up work concentrates mainly on the particular training unit at the time, which can vary considerably – technique, running practice, tactics etc.

The match, on the other hand, demands from the very outset, 100% fitness of one's whole psycho-physical constitution. Therefore, it deserves its own special kind of warming-up programme.

Soccer is a team game conducted by individuals and thus ruled by two principles: on the one hand, the sporting event is determined by the physical and mental attitude and loading capacity of the individual; on the other hand, the working together as a team is an important contributory factor towards the desired success. Any shortcomings in the physical and mental attitude of an individual player affects the harmony of the whole team, and that also applies to the attitude to warming-up and warming-down.

1.1 Physiological Aspects of Warming-up

Whilst looking for further arguments in favour of warming-up, the following list from DE MAREES/MESTER has proved useful:

▶ **Increasing the muscle and body temperature**
Warming-up leads to a specific increase in body temperature ranging from 38.5-39.5° Celsius, whereby the muscle temperature rises fairly fast in the first five minutes, whilst the body temperature increases gradually over about 30 minutes. As far as performance ability is concerned, muscle temperature is the more important factor.

▶ **Accelerating the metabolic process**
Wherever muscles are at work there is a greater need of energy. Phosphate-rich energy supplies, which are momentarily available in reserve but must be replaced immediately, replenish the stores. By warming-up gradually one achieves a more intense aerobic supply of energy and thus protects the anaerobic reserves of energy. Thus the lactate levels remain lower during intense exercise (lactate = salt of lactic acid and is a waste product of anaerobic oxidation). A great increase in lactate levels causes overoxidation of the muscles and consequently reduces performance ability.
The increased need of oxygen as a result of exercise is not only supplied by increased blood circulation through the affected muscles, but a more effective use of the amount of oxygen in the blood follows.

▶ **Increasing the performance ability of the nervous system**

If the body temperature rises, then the speed at which nerve impulses are transferred also increases. Specific warming-up improves one's co-ordinating ability in performance, creates a good feeling of mobility and increases both one's overall perception and alertness.

Warming-up influences the nervous system, optimises perception and reactions and is thus a prerequisite for success in certain technical matters.

Therefore, room should be made for specific sporting mobility sequences during any warming-up programme.

▶ **Raising the speed of muscle contraction**

Systematic warming-up increases the working muscle's ability to absorb oxygen, improves its working speed and so makes it more effective. It also leads to increased mobility, lower consumption of energy, greater joint mobility and lower risk of injury. Furthermore, it helps the working muscles to relax better, which is just as important for quick and precise movements, as well as cyclic-endurance sequences of movement.

▶ **Reducing the risk of injury in the long-term to muscles, ligaments and tendons**

Reducing the risk of injury by warming-up is not just applicable to specific cases but also the so-called "later reactions" to performance-orientated sport. This applies particularly to competitive games during which the player's muscles, ligaments and tendons are put under extreme loads both at the outset and towards the end of a game, when the player is exhausted.

▶ **Reducing stress on the joints**

Peter KNEBEL has proved that optimum elasticity and plasticity of the collagenous fibres is first reached with a temperature of 39°C. This statement is significant for all kinds of stretching and other mechanical stresses. If one assumes that the joint cartilage's ability to nourish itself improves by movement, then exercises should be included in the warming-up programme, which positively stimulate the cartilage of the joints and inter-vertebral discs. Running involves almost all the joints.

At this stage it is significant that precise technique during the mobility sequences, and also when training with the ball, is an important requisite for reducing load on the joints. Each incorrect technical performance can cause over-, or wrong, stress on the mobility organs. Mobility sequences which are technically out of harmony with each other require more effort and exertion as well as leading to a reduction of endurance performance.

▶ Reducing the initial O_2 deficits

MAEHL∕HÖHNKE state that: "The increased metabolic rate brought about by warming-up ensures better delivery of and better use of oxygen, as well as faster removal of carbon dioxide and other waste products." Warming-up leads to much better blood circulation up to six times the starting rate, and also helps to get rid of abrasive irritants in the working muscles. The breathing rate adapts to increased use and becomes faster and deeper. In a fully-trained player it is mainly the volume of each breath which is increased, whereas in an untrained player the breathing frequency rises.

The wrong kind of warming-up development

▶ Just as when starting a car too quickly you can damage the engine in the longer term, so also can warming-up too fast lead to a premature use of energy which could be needed later.

▶ Warming-up too fast can prevent the body's reaching the temperature it needs to ensure good performance because the human body takes time to absorb and transform physiological and psychological stimuli.

▶ If warming-up in a way suited to each type of sport is not adapted to the subsequent demands of performance, then reaching the desired goal is made more difficult or restricted.

1.2 Psychological Aspects of Warming-up

During the warming-up stage, physical and psychological aspects stand alongside each other. On the one hand, warming-up aims at alertness and being active, motivates one for learning situations and awakens the desire to be sportively active; on the other hand, this stage is also responsible for creating tension and relaxation, and eradicating over-involvement.

Psychomotoric activity, emotional stimulation and, in team sports, the social aspects are described in the following words: "readiness to attack, willingness to participate, active tension, alertness, tension, being loosened up, attentiveness".

And so a trainer should know the following when involved in warming-up with his players:

▶ The warming-up should be stimulating and varied, so that it does not look like some kind of bluff to the players.
▶ Any pressure on the players can be reduced by movement.
▶ Any particular preplay tension in the players can be released by movement and game-simulating activities.
▶ Establishing the most positive attitude possible is the best guarantee for a favourable expectant start.
▶ Good preparation gives the player his own personal feeling of security.

In performance sport, the player consciously aims for a positive and desirable stress situation before the game begins. When dealing with less motivated players, the trainer can specifically increase this or reduce it in overmotivated players.

1.2.1 Mental Training

Mental training is "the systematic, intensive, mental concept of a scheme of movement without any simultaneous practical execution, aimed at improving the scheme of movement (inner realisation)" as defined by Peter RÖTHIG. Thus, mental training primarily helps to improve sporting skills, which are aimed at co-ordination or contain a range of movements. So this is suited to being combined with practical training.

Mental training aims at optimising technical and dynamic schemes of movement, by a conscious mental idea of the movements. A pattern of movement develops which the co-ordinating aspects can improve on during real movement practice. So it is not enough to just think about how to move, you actually need to do it!

Thus, mental training becomes a part of active warming-up, but only has any point during automatised schemes of movement if enough information is available about the movement.

When preparing oneself mentally for a game, goals are important such as freeing the sportsman from any distractions and problem situations outside the game, so that his concentration on the specific task-in-hand increases and it is then possible to produce positive feelings and associations. Therefore any defeats in the past three years against an opposing team must be turned into positive energy by setting oneself realistic goals.

1.2.2 Psychoregulative Training

Hans SCHELLENBERGER describes psychoregulative training as follows: "The main aim of all psychoregulative proceedings is to relax and mobilise the sportsman. Its effectiveness depends on the close connection between the higher centres of the central nervous system (thinking and speaking processes and powers of imagination) and the vegetative functions and ideomotoric reactions. The psychical influence on the organism can be learnt. The psychoregulative effect lies in taking energy from the cells of the nervous system."

The psychoregulative relaxation procedure has three methods:

▶ autogenious training
▶ psychotonic training
▶ concentrated relaxation training

Psychoregulative activation on the other hand has five possible methods:

▶ ideomotoric training
▶ mental training
▶ observative training
▶ formalised planning or project building
▶ desensibilisation

Without going into any further detail here, the interested reader can consult appropriate literature on the subject. In summing up, the following is important: the aim of psychoregulative training is to guide the factors of person, situation and task in such a way as to bring them into proper union favourably with each other.

One must also realise that the trainer in a team game must work in a "double-tracked" way. On the one hand he must direct his main work towards the whole team, on the other hand he needs a fully developed preparation programme with regard to a psychoregulative attitude for each individual player.

1.2.3 Social Aspects

Soccer as a team sport is directed towards playing together and competing with each other. When getting ready for a game in small groups within the framework of warming-up, for example, social contacts with each other are specifically trained to ensure the necessary feel for the game. However, it is just as important to practise duelling situations, in order to be able to succeed in the game. It is essential that each player quickly finds his own rhythm for the game, so that the whole team can achieve their desired performance level.

2 WARMING-UP FROM A METHODICAL TRAINING POINT OF VIEW

Before addressing types and methods of warming-up, certain influencing factors should be clarified:

▶ **The player's training condition**

The better trained the player is, the more intensive the warming-up phase. But a warming-up programme is indispensable at all levels of performance. In addition to this, the individual requirements which each player brings with him play a decisive role e.g. someone with a muscular injury must take special care with stretching exercises, but in order to create the very best level of performance more time must be spent on stretching.

WARMING-UP – EACH IN LINE WITH HIS OWN LEVEL OF PERFORMANCE

▶ **Age of the players**

Systematic warming-up suitable for each type of sport whether, in top performance or general sport, is indispensable for all age-groups from about the age of twelve. For children below this age limit, it is hardly necessary to warm-up for physical reasons. But it would appear that, from a long-term teaching point it is an acceptable argument to bring children into contact with the idea of warming-up as playfully as possible.

WARMING-UP – A MUST FOR YOUNG AND OLD

▶ **External factors**

The player must be familiar with all the outside conditions like: situation of the sports ground, the state of the ground, weather, spectators, time of day and many other factors.

WARMING-UP – ADJUSTING TO EXTERNAL INFLUENCES

▶ **Length of warming-up**

In order to reach the necessary muscle temperature for top performance sport, fifteen minutes of warming-up is probably sufficient, but training experts regard a warming-up time of up to 30 minutes necessary for a match, and also correct with regard to the right body temperature. There should be a maximum of five to ten minutes between the end of the warming-up stage and the beginning of the demands of performance.

Experts often bemoan in the current situation that a much too intensive, and therefore foreshortened, warming-up for soccer, can lead to overstraining the working muscles and possibly the danger of cramps. One should also avoid lack of practice situations whilst warming-up.

WARMING-UP TAKES TIME

▶ **Intensity of warming-up**

The warming-up programme can start with 50% involvement and gradually increase to 80%. If it is too intense, willingness to perform dwindles and robs the player of strength, speed and endurance when he is playing. If the warming-up work on the other hand is too lax, the necessary strength of performance is absent from the game, especially in extreme situations.

A slow and steady increase can indicate to the player himself that he has chosen the right amount of warming-up. A further indication comes from economising the metabolic process by more favourable breathing equivalence and an increase in the ability to absorb oxygen. Finally, the player's mobility increases, technical and playful activities are accomplished in a better co-ordinated way, and his nervous system can control and play past obstacles more securely.

WARMING-UP – A WAY OF GETTING INTO THE GAME

▶ **Choice of exercises**

Within the range of chosen exercises for warming-up, one must take both physiological unhesitating behaviour into consideration as much as effectiveness. At the same time, partner exercises and readily available manual equipment can strengthen the team's spirit in any kind of team sport. Whilst warming-up, the real bit of sports apparatus, the ball, can accompany the players as often as possible, because its use acts as motivation.

Warming-up before training can be directed towards a specific learning goal and should contain this kind of emphasis somewhere. On the other hand, when preparing directly for a match, the players work to a standard programme, which is specially adapted towards their individual disposition and their unique tasks in the game.

▶ **Motivation, experience and independence**

Many a player runs through the warming-up stage before playing and training, more because he has to, than out of a sense of conviction, and because he has not yet experienced any advantages in doing it. If he is going to be better motivated towards the preparation stage, so that he internalises the need to warm up for himself, then he must see, some value in it. Only then can warming-up become an obvious and independently desirable component in training and competition.

WARMING-UP – ONE MUST EXPERIENCE IT FOR ONESELF

▶ **Special case, reserve players**

Two different ways of bringing reserves onto the field can occur in a game i.e. one planned and the other dependent on the situation. In both cases, the same starting point can be adhered to: both players have done some intensive warming-up before the game starts.

If the planned exchange is allowed, the new player can be prepared for playing again by a temporarily shortened programme suited to the sporting situation.

On the other hand, changing independent of the situation e.g. because of injury to a fellow player, rarely permits warming-up suitable for the competitive situation. And yet some basic kind of warming-up is available.

This should be refreshed again and again during the course of the game by a kind of "after warming". Therefore it is a good idea if trainers send their reserve players to warm up from time to time, even if this suggestion does not exactly thrill them, especially if they are not called onto the field.

WARMING-UP – PREPARED TO PLAY AT ANYTIME

2.1 Warming-up Methods

There are two ways of setting about warming-up: active and passive. Active warming-up demands individual activity, whereas passive comes about via massage, hot showers, warm baths and time in the sauna. You cannot prepare sufficiently for the demands of training and certainly not matches, with passive forms of warming-up alone.

However, they can be granted a supporting role which, for practical reasons, are more favourable for warming-down from the demands of performance than preparing for it.

2.2 Ways of Warming-up

Active warming-up is divided into various categories within the specialised literature, which follow on from each other according to level and order. Alongside general books, one can find special warming-up with exercises directed towards specific sports, stretching, stretching and strengthening gymnastics, as well as co-ordinative tuning. Individual warming-up completes all aforementioned forms.

▶ General warming-up helps to increase one's body temperature, activates the heart and circulatory system, as well as the psychical tuning in to the approaching activity. The large blocks of muscles and the whole body are warmed up by trotting, running, running gymnastics and whole body gymnastics.

▶ Special warming-up mainly pursues goals for specific kinds of sport and is directed towards strength, power, endurance, technique and tactics, and strengthens one's co-ordinating ability. Here especially muscles under a lot of strain are specially prepared by stretching and strengthening exercises. By alternating between short sprints and endurance running with and without the ball, playing in and playing at competitive situations ease the way into the game.

▶ Individual warming-up, as its name suggests, can only be done in small groups or with individual players. As there are many different reasons for individual warming-up, it is impossible here to give any idea of length of time or content. The actual content for this particular need is determined by the occasion. So, for example, after a long period of injury, or hardening of an affected muscle, an additional amount of warming-up or stretching is required which is increased slowly.

In the following chart an attempt has been made to present the main aims and their accompanying ways of realising the warming-up process. It must be pointed out however that warming-up work today, prior to training and match, no longer rigidly adheres to this structure. The individual stages of warming-up proceed smoothly one after the other and combine to give a warming-up procedure which the experienced player can adjust to his own personality.

Warming-up Structure

Main aims		Realisation
• Stimulating heart and circulatory activity • Increasing basic body temperature • Warming-up large groups of muscles • Preparation for imminent psychical stress	general warming-up 10-15 minutes	• Easy trotting and running oneself warm • Whole body exercises • Co-ordination exercises
• Preparation of the muscles and nervous system for the demands of specific sports (strength, power, endurance, technique, tactics, co-ordination) • Optimising the psychical tuning in	specific warming-up 10-15 minutes	• Stretching, stretching exercises for stabilising the mobility apparatus • Strengthening muscles under particular strain. • Dynamic co-ordination exercises for building up an optimum interplay of muscle and nerve • Speed exercises • Playing in and playing through competitive situations
• Improving individual weaknesses • Building up again after injury and longer gaps in play • Consideration of one's conditional disposition or state of mind	individual warming-up	• Stretching of shortened muscles • Strengthening of weak muscles • Special demands in the match

Once more, the aim and objective of warming-up and warming-down, important to be gained from training, needs to be clarified.

1. One needs to impress on each player how vitally important warming-up and warming-down is.

2. The player should be familiar with the exercises and types of movement involved in warming-up and warming-down, and be able to use them for himself and other people.

3. The player must feel the effect on his own body and performance ability and have a positive attitude towards it all.

4. Finally, the player must be in a position to warm up himself to suit his own needs and the demands put on him.

2.3 Warming-up in Line with the Main Demands on the Player

Various kinds of motoric demands can lie at the centre of a soccer training unit. Warming-up can be directed mainly towards this situation. Preparation for training of a **technical** nature primarily demands the mobilisation of co-ordinative suppositions.

Thus, various elements of specific patterns of movement are to be found in the warming-up programme, which on the one hand prepare the core of the training unit, and on the other hand pave the way for patterns of movement in a future programme.

Warming-up procedures before **strength training** – as far as soccer is concerned usually muscle strength work – are likewise strengthened by activating one's co-ordinative skill and ability to react. In this way, later mobility issues can be practised in advance by several repeats of lesser intensity.

If the warming-up is to lead to greater demand for **speed**, then raising the muscle temperature is particularly effective. Gymnastics and stretching exercises of varying intensity and including loosening up, which are directed towards particular sports and are both constantly strengthening and dynamic, achieve the desired raising of muscle temperature and thus prepare for improved speed. Therefore, it is important to include such elements as short sprints in the player's warming-up programme, so that he can cope with the main emphasis of training better i.e. demands of speed. Take note that warming-up too intensively or too fast can create exhaustion and have a negative influence on the reaction and contraction of one's muscles.

Soccer demands **endurance** from the player. Warming-up before the training point "endurance" is reached, increases slowly, so that aerobic energy can be gained better and anaerobic reserves stored up for later. By specific warming-up the player produces solid lactate supplies within the main stress period and can thus succeed better for example in running duels.

2.4 Stretching and Strengthening

From the following two diagrams of the most important human muscle groups, one can see which muscles play a decisive role in soccer:

Important Muscles of the Human Skeleton

Front view

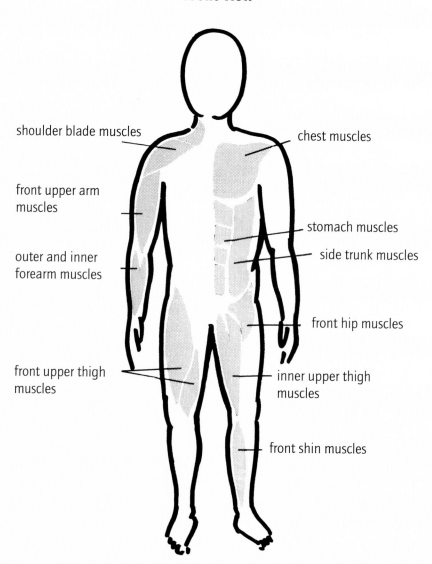

shoulder blade muscles

front upper arm
muscles

outer and inner
forearm muscles

front upper thigh
muscles

chest muscles

stomach muscles

side trunk muscles

front hip muscles

inner upper thigh
muscles

front shin muscles

Back view

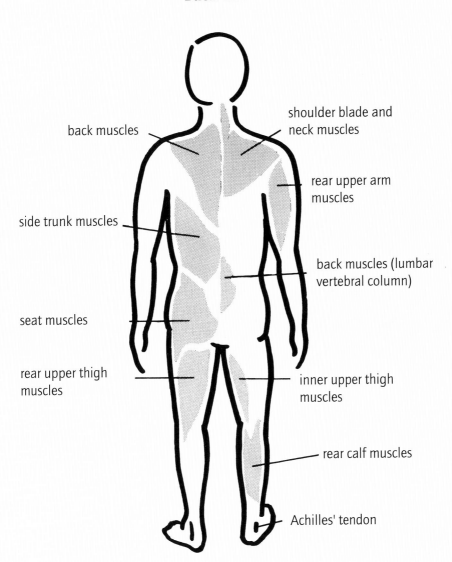

back muscles

shoulder blade and neck muscles

rear upper arm muscles

side trunk muscles

back muscles (lumbar vertebral column)

seat muscles

rear upper thigh muscles

inner upper thigh muscles

rear calf muscles

Achilles' tendon

If a soccer player is to be prepared in the best way possible for the main part of his training or a match, then all parts of his muscles must first be well warmed-up and mobilised. Yet certain muscles like hip or leg muscles need special attention as they determine all the course of movement during a soccer match. When heading a ball, naturally neck and stomach muscles are also involved.

When warming-up for soccer, the following muscle groups should be specially stretched:
S =   Stretch: muscles which are inclined to contract must be stretched
S 4   Shoulder and neck muscles
        The contraction of this group of muscles causes neck ache. Avoid circling the head during stretching exercises.
S 6   Side trunk muscles
        A hollow back occurs during contraction.
S 7   Back muscles in the lumbar vertebral section
        Contraction also leads to a hollow back and to backache.
S 9   Inner upper thigh muscles
        Contraction causes groin problems. When doing stretching exercises here, stretch the knee.
S 10   Rear upper thigh muscles
        Stretching reduces the danger of straining.
S 11   Front upper thigh and hip vertebrae muscles
        A lot of sitting contracts the muscle and causes lower backache.
S 12   Rear calf muscles: Stretching reduces Achilles' tendon problems.

During warming-up for soccer, the following groups of muscles should be strengthened:
Str.=   Strengthen: muscles inclined to show weakness must be strengthened.
Str. 4   Shoulder blade and neck muscles
        Strengthening helps prevent a rounded back.
Str. 8   Seat muscle
        Strengthening establishes a stable pelvis.
Str. 10 Rear upper thigh muscles
        Strengthening balances kneebending and stretching i.e. extensor and flexor muscles.
Str. 11 Front upper thigh muscles
        The knee joints are stabilized by stretching.
Str. 13 Stomach muscles
        If the trunk is stabilised then the maximum amount of strength is released.
Str. 14 Back muscles in the chest vertebrae section
        One counteracts the danger of a rounded back.
Str. 15 Front shin muscles: The ankle is stabilised by strengthening.

And the following should also be noted when stretching and strengthening:

- ▶ Players need self-discipline if the stretching and strengthening of a warming-up programme are to be really effective. You can only have the desired effect if you take the trouble to exercise properly.
- ▶ Stretching and strengthening exercises are constantly supplemented with loosening-up exercises.
- ▶ When tired, stretching and strengthening can only be done gently, otherwise there is risk of injury.
- ▶ Similarly, the individual condition of the sportsman plays a decisive role in deciding how intensely, and how many times, the exercises should be carried out.
- ▶ Avoid any sort of strained breathing whilst exercising.
- ▶ Muscle groups subjected to special strain, need intensive if not special warming-up.
- ▶ Stretching and strengthening usually take place after general warming-up.
- ▶ Flexor and extensor muscles are equally trained, so that the tension ratio of the muscles is maintained.
- ▶ With beginners and young people, the stretching and strengthening exercises should be built up systematically and gradually.
- ▶ Exercise times for stretching and strengthening are slowly increased.
- ▶ When warming-up one is not so much concerned with the amount of exercise but rather that it is all conducted accurately.

2.5 Ten Tips for Planning a Warming-up Session

1. Warming-up involves trotting as well as running and relaxation after muscular stress.

2. Warming-up is built up step by step and initially avoids any types of exercise which are too intensive or stressful.

3. The key feature for the following training unit can be revealed during the course of warming-up (contact with the vital theme by use of apparatus, similarity of exercise etc.).

4. The chosen exercises should be mastered by all players if possible.

5. Co-ordination exercises should be done on both sides (feet, hands etc.).

6. As insight motivates, the players should see the point of the exercise.

7. Before any tense groups of muscles are strengthened, stretching exercises should be done.

8. Each player must determine his own level and dose of individual stress.

9. When warming-up the trainer should work to the simple principle of demonstrating everything.

10. Avoid the following exercises if possible: uncontrolled circling of the head, too much load on neck as when doing a head stand or shoulder stand, too much load with very long lever effect e.g. from outstretched legs, too much lively swinging movement from a stretching position, and overloading the knees when bending below 90° as if doing a Cossack dance crouching down low.

3 OBSERVATIONS ON THE WARMING-UP PROGRAMMES

Proper warming-up, that is getting oneself in the right mood for the main part of the training or for a match does not only work to prevent injury, but also prepares the players physically, psychologically, motivationally and psycho-socially for the exertions ahead of them. One is actually concerned with supplying the activists with the necessary background knowledge, and thereby not only to motivate them, but above all to impart information with regard to "warming-up". At all times the paramount aim should be to make them capable of organising their own warming-up. In particular, if one manages to get children and young people used to this then it can have lasting effect when faced with such tasks.

It is important for both trainers and players that they are aware of the basic structures of arranging warming-up programmes, so that they can be sensibly changed or altered: but day-to-day practise in the soccer clubs is that much more flexible and replaceable, so that plenty of variation can be brought into the warming-up processes. For example, stretching can retreat into the background from time to time, if dynamic gymnastic exercises for strengthening and improving mobility have priority instead. Instead of a period of running in, there could be a warming-up game in a small group but without introducing any competitive concept.

As the warming-up programme continues, more attention is given to specifically competitive exercises, games and other game features e.g. sprints on the touch-line, shots at goal from various positions, like headed balls in a one-on-one situation, and small games of three against three or five against five. Certain features of the game are practised in advance, which will play an important role during the course of the game, according to one's own tactics. In this way the players gradually grow into coping with the necessary stresses and strains of competition.

The "stretching euphoria" around in the early 1980s has cooled down to a more realistic level. Stretching gymnastics still undoubtedly occupies an important place in the whole process of training and preparation for a match, as stretching exercises improve, above all else, the player's mobility and counteract the tendency to contract certain muscles. Demanding and combined patterns of movement are thus learnt and mastered more easily. On the other hand, after basic warming-up, the stretching exercises can be incorporated into almost all parts of the warming-up programme.

Trainers, on the whole, rarely stick to the prescribed theoretical structure of warming-up. They work with a mixture of methods in order to avoid monotony. The use of simple manual apparatus like ropes, batons, medicine balls etc. can help in the same way, but warming-up in pairs or in a small group can likewise create similar variety. The most important piece of „manual apparatus", the ball should, however, never be forgotten. Indeed, it should be part of the warming-up process as often as possible. In lower grades, with little time to spare for training, the trainer must understand the particular situation of the players. The little time available for training and often poor technique are good reasons for combining special warming-up with coaching in technique. But the trainer should always bear the following in mind: the players are also looking to enjoy their training!

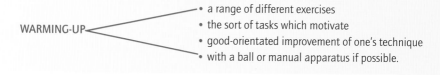

WARMING-UP

- a range of different exercises
- the sort of tasks which motivate
- good-orientated improvement of one's technique
- with a ball or manual apparatus if possible.

Once the players have absorbed the warming-up process and chosen it to be a permanent part of their training and match programme, then the development is nearing its goal. The trainer can then give the players 10-15 minutes for general warming-up on their own. Just the special warming-up time, in so far as the desired aim requires it, remaining under his leadership.

4 WARMING-UP PROGRAMME

The following warming-up programmes are aimed at individual players, partners and small groups i.e. teams. They are devised for use with and without a ball, with a medicine ball and with skipping ropes. The two latter pieces of manual apparatus serve as an excellent incentive for the trainer to build other simple bits of manual apparatus into the warming-up.

4.1 Ten Warming-up Programmes for Individual Players (1-10)

Innumerable types of warming-up movements are just right for the individual sportsman. But that does not exclude practising alongside each other, helping, one another or working in the same rhythm as one's neighbour.

Warming-up PROGRAMME 1 with Ball

General warming-up

- Each player dribbles the ball lightly.
- The ball is juggled in the air.
- Direction and speed are altered whilst dribbling the ball.
- The ball is juggled again for as long as possible.
- The ball is kicked along with the right and then left outside foot.
- More ball juggling.
- Each player sprints after the ball as it is played along in front of him.

Special warming-up

Strengthening the stomach muscles
From a lengthened sitting position one leg is bent and raised. The ball is passed under the bent knee from the right hand into the left hand.

Strengthening the adductors
From a sitting position with both legs bent at an angle, the ball is pressed between the knees.

Mobilizing the trunk
The ball is rolled in figures of eight round the legs, which are apart.

Graded runs with ball
During a graded run, the ball is first kicked with the right and then with the left foot.

Relaxation
Each player loosens up and shakes out arms and legs.

Graded runs with ball
During the running, a sign is given for changing the direction through 180°.

Warming-up PROGRAMME 2 with Ball

General warming-up

- At a relaxed trotting speed the ball is kicked first with the right and then with the left foot.
- The ball is kicked alternately with the inside and outside of the foot.
- After throwing the ball up high, the player takes it and dribbles it further.
- The player throws the ball up very high, does a forward roll, takes the ball and carries on dribbling.
- Whilst dribbling, the player stops the ball with the sole of his foot and carries on playing.
- The player throws the ball up high, heads it forwards lightly, catches it with his foot, flips it up with his foot, heads it again and repeats.

Special warming-up

Limbering up
In a standing position, the ball is guided round the hips, whereby the hips make circular movements.

Limbering up
Whilst lying on one's back, raise seat and trunk and roll the ball under one's bottom.

Relaxation
Whilst lying on one's back, give the legs a good shake.

Strengthening
From a press-ups position, bounce the ball alternately with left and right hand.

Strengthening
From a press-ups position on one arm throw the ball up a little way and catch it.

Playing in
In small groups the ball is passed to each other whilst moving and only a short distance apart.

Warming-up PROGRAMME 3 with Ball

General warming-up

Using cones, a square is marked out with each side 30-40 metres long.

- Each player dribbles the ball round the square at a gentle speed.
- Whilst dribbling round the square with the ball, the speed is increased along two parallel sides.
- The players separate out at the four corner cones. When told to, they dribble across the square, but without touching each other when they reach the middle.
- Each player does a few stretching exercises familiar to him.
- Two groups are formed. Group A balances the ball inside the square, and group B dribbles round the square with the ball. The exercise is repeated with the groups changed over.
- Whilst going round the square, each player puts the ball down along one side of the square and sprints after it.

Special warming-up

Stretching
Whilst doing the splits, the ball is rolled to left and right. Stop briefly at each end position.

Stretching
From a lengthened sitting position, the ball is rolled round the stretched out legs and seat.

Playing in
At top speed, play centre passes from left or right in front of the goal.

Playing in
Balls are raised in front of the goal and headed towards the goal.

Playing in
An opposing player is dribbled past with the ball.

Speed
The player puts the ball in front of him, sprints after it and shoots at the goal.

Warming-up PROGRAMME 4 with Ball

General warming-up

Two squares (10 x 10 metres) are marked out with cones, 20 to 30 metres apart.
- All the players dribble the ball in square A. When the trainer indicates, they change to square B (no competition).
- The players move about dribbling the ball between the two squares. The trainer calls out a word (e.g. offside). If the word has an even number of letters, the player change to square A, and if an uneven number to square B.
- The ball should be kept in the air by the players and sent from square A to square B.
- The ball is propelled by a bow-shot from square A to B. The players sprint after it and take it before it reaches the ground a second time.
- Each player completes a few gymnastic exercises with his own ball.

Special warming-up

Stretching
With legs stretched, the player tilts the upper part of his body forwards.

Stretching
The player sits crouching low down, arms above his knees and feet flat on the ground.

Flexibility
The ball is bounced with right and left hand alternately, whilst the player slowly descends into a crouching position.

Strengthening
Lying on one's back with the ball on the feet. By lifting the legs, the ball rolls towards the chin and by lifting the upper part of one's body, the ball rolls back to the feet.

Relaxation
Arms and legs are shaken out whilst running around.

Playing in
Duelling behaviour is practiced in a one against one game.

Warming-up PROGRAMME 5

General warming-up

- The players run and limber up without a ball this time.
- They run forwards and backwards.
- They add skipping and side-galloping to their running.
- After that the arms are loosened up.
- Circle the arms and dangle them whilst running.
- The upper part of the body hangs forwards and is loosened up.
- To strengthen their leg muscles, the players hop on the spot with both legs and then with left or right foot.
- The legs are shaken out.
- Players turn on their own axis whilst running around.
- The players sit on the floor and loosen up arms and legs.

Special warming-up

Stretching the inner upper thigh muscles
Right and left leg are stretched out sideways alternately.

Stretching the rear calf muscles
The player stands with feet apart and both feet flat on the floor, whilst the hip is pushed forward.

Stretching the rear upper thigh muscles
The player steps out, bending the back leg and stretching the front one.

Co-ordination
The player stands balancing on one leg.

Playing in
Within the 16 metres area the team plays catch, whereby three catchers must catch the rest of the team. Whoever is caught, juggles the ball.

Playing in
Balls played at low level from left or right are shot towards the goal.

Warming-up PROGRAMME 6

General warming-up

To begin with, only running exercises without the ball.

- The players gradually run themselves warm and consciously bend and stretch their ankles.
- Trotting around is accompanied by arm-circling.
- Now the players add a few gymnastic exercises to their running programme, whilst all the players run one behind the other, and the team captain demonstrates the movements.
- Whilst running raise the knees for 15-20 metres at a time.
- Whilst the players are running around, the trainer calls out instructions to crouch, kneel or lie down.

Special warming-up

Ensure that time is left for relaxation in between stretching and strengthening exercises.

Stretching the muscles of the lower back and seat
The player lies on his back with legs pulled up and then rocks.

Stretching the hip-bending muscles
Whilst kneeling on one knee, the hip is brought forward.

Stretching the adductors
Sitting cross-legged the player presses his knees towards the ground.

Strengthening the shoulders
Kneeling on one leg, supported on one arm, the other arm, back and leg are in line with each other.

Strengthening the back muscles
Lying on one's stomach, right arm and left leg are raised slightly.

Playing in
One pair of players at a time sprints after a ball kicked by the trainer and tries by tackling to get it for himself.

Warming-up PROGRAMME 7

General warming-up

- The players run themselves in slowly by trotting.
- They run on tiptoe or on their heels.
- They kick their heels against their bottom whilst running.
- We now insert a few whole body exercises, to be done as each player thinks fit.
- Whilst still running round, the players jump into the air and try to stay there as long as possible.
- All players run one behind the other and, when the word is given, the last player in line runs to the front.
- Whilst running in different directions (north, south, east and west), the trainer calls out the direction for a 15 metre sprint for the players. In between times, the players just trot around.

Special warming-up

Stretching the hip-joint bending muscles and calf muscles

The players make a fall-out step with the back leg stretched out and the pelvis pushed forward. The rear heel is actively pushed onto the ground.

Stretching the knee-joint stretching muscles

From a kneeling position, pull the rear foot towards one's bottom, by which the hip is pushed forward keeping the back straight.

Stretching the bottom muscles and hip-bending muscles on the other side
Whilst lying on one's back, one leg is pulled up and the other actively kept on the ground.

Strengthening the straight and transverse stomach muscles
Whilst lying on one's back, both legs are held at an angle of 90°. The shoulder blades are lifted slightly.

Strengthening the side trunk muscles
Do a press-up to one side on your elbow, whilst simultaneously raising your pelvis.

Playing in
Two players at a time kick high balls towards each other, playing the ball as directly as possible and without keeping it.

Warming-up PROGRAMME 8

General warming-up

- The players start trotting gently.
- Skipping is brought into the trotting movement.
- Each player does a few whole body exercises on his own.
- Run sideways turning one's upper body.
- During skipping both arms are specifically used.
- From a position of lying on one's back or stomach do a few sprints when told to.
- Three players at a time play vaulting.
- In the 16 metre area, the four corners receive the number 1-4. The trainer calls out combinations of numbers (e.g. 143) and each player must run past the corners in that order of numbers.

Special training

Ensure that you relax after each stretching and strengthening exercise.

Stretching the adductor muscles
From a standing position, the body weight is transferred to one side. If the right leg is outstretched, one's weight is to the left and vice versa.

Stretching the underarm stretching muscle
The right arm is bent behind your head, and then the left hand is used to pull the right elbow backwards.

Strengthening the stomach muscles
Lying on your back with legs pulled up at an angle, raise your shoulder blades and upper body slightly.

Strengthening the bottom muscles
From a bench-type position, each leg is raised at an angle of 90° alternately.

Co-ordination
The player stands on one leg swinging the other leg simultaneously, whilst also circling his arms.

Playing in
The player imitates dribbling with fast attack and feinting.

Warming-up PROGRAMME 9 with a Skipping Rope

General warming-up

Each player has a skipping rope.
- With the rope the players trot lightly across the sports ground.
- During warming-up by running, the rope is swung to left and right beside one's body.
- Whilst running, try skipping with one, two or three steps between skips.
- The rope is shortened and then jumped over.
- One player swings the rope briefly over the ground. The others jump over the rope.
- Whilst running, the rope is thrown up as high as possible and caught again.
- The players skip on the spot, getting their legs as high as possible into the air.

Special warming-up

Gymnastic exercise
The rope is held fairly short. With legs apart, the arms are raised and one's upper body turned to left and right. Hold the final position briefly.

Gymnastic exercise
The rope is held fairly short. With legs apart and arms raised, the upper body is tilted sideways.